The Little Swimmer

Written by **Grandma Susie**

Illustrated by **Hannah H. Dayton**

This story is dedicated to all the little
swimmers
who will grow up...

like my beautiful granddaughter Gigi...
And swim like a fish!

When I was really, really, little...

I could not swim by myself.
Mommy or Daddy had to help me in
the pool.

And at the beach...to keep me safe!
Do NOT go near the water by
yourself.

You need to learn how to SWIM!

Sometimes I put on my swimmies!

You have to keep your mouth closed!
You might swallow water....YUCK!

Once, I forgot !
I was laughing and splashing!
GULP!!

I wish...
I was a FISH!
Fish can swim all by themselves!

But...I am not a fish .
You are not a fish either.
We would look pretty silly!!

GUESS WHAT ???

I am learning how to KICK my feet!

I am learning how to MOVE my arms!

I am learning how to HOLD my BREATH!

I am learning how to SWIM!

I am bigger now...and you will grow

And learn to swim, too!!

GUESS WHAT ???
I can swim like a FISH!

I am a SWIMMER!

About the Illustrator:

Hannah Dayton, the Illustrator, is a talented 19 year old artist that loves bringing her various characters and stories to life through art. She really believes that Art is a gift that is meant to be shared!

When she isn't drawing, she loves to explore the outdoors or read a good book. She is currently attending Southern Connecticut State University to study Art Education, and is planning on becoming an art teacher one day. "The Little Swimmer" is her first venture into the world of illustrating children's books.